EVERYWHERE I AM

EVERY WHERE I AM

EVERYWHERE I AM

Arden Z Heller, Jr.

Scythe Publications, Inc.

A Division of Winston-Derek Publishers Group, Inc.

PUBLISHED BY SCYTHE PUBLICATIONS, INC.
A Division of Winston-Derek Publishers Group, Inc.
Nashville, Tennessee 37228

Library of Congress Catalog Card No: 96-060621
ISBN: 1-55523-801-7

Printed in the United States of America

for Mother and the Muses

Table of Contents

THIS DREAM

THIS DREAM...

I had this dream, see
what a dream!
black and white
and color scheme

what a dream!
You were there

What a sight:
of baby blue
the sky was hued
of black and white
the people

in this dream what... thoughts did mean
i still don't dare to venture

Water roared and licked with foam
whiter than all of whiteness
waves climbed high, then
fell from the sky
as raindrops in a shower

there was this sign which read:
    LIFE POURS AS WINE

    COME FILL YOUR HEAD

This island was all ours
and for those, like us, lost in thoughts of dreaming
as we stared at nature's flare
we didn't dare to venture

We stood still through time's repeal
(do you remember how it felt?)
with twilight's blend we saw *the end*

and how it went on forever
and time stood still, but what the hell!
(as i say) we were here forever!

In the building on the island
began the genocide
conveyor belts
that reached the heavens
never touched the sky

man! we were like so much cattle
(but we lead ourselves astray)
no one was in charge of us
still, we played the game

it seemed to be the thing to do:
damn yourself to hell!
the newest craze in sporting games
for the masochist – a sell!

Somehow i broke free of this
and hovered through the air
through the roof, into the darkness
and watched you from midair

i could see right through the building
saw you standing there
i called to you
(though in my mind)
but you didn't seem to care!

Yeah, it was a dream
(or so it seemed)
am i *here* or sleeping *there*?

you were there... you tell me!

NONSENSE- NUMBER ONE

You were there … i saw you there!
i tried to get to you
everywhere! … you *were* there
i couldn't get to you

I followed you throughout the night
though it was light as day
but then again, how could i know
for inside we did stay

It was a building long and wide
(a warehouse of a sort)
but this seemed much *much* more equipped
for those who practice sports

Stairs without steps to climb
were slidden down then up
up the banister (used for a handhold)
up and up and up!

a grasp! a pull! a tug!
again! again! again! until the end
i reached the top!
i reached it!
i would win!

Having done so, i slid me down
before i stood me up!
and having done this – twice or thrice – my mind
had had enough!

I continued searching: Here and There
High and Low in Circles

you weren't there – anywhere!
around and around i circled

With an eye, i caught you high
Up and Down you went
you'd hoist yourself as if yourself
were just a sack now spent

Slick, unbent your movements went each time
you chinned you up
Up and Down without a sound – you didn't even grunt!
You caught my eye, your friends did spy me
and peered at me abruptly
before i called, you chinned *Your All*
then vanished with a – poof!

I was alone as i did roam
shadows gaped around me
across the walls
they Creeped! they Crawled!
and stepped about – though lightly

Not a sound marked the ground
not a tap or scraping
but they were there – everywhere!
their silence Bellowed soundly

Next in line, i marked some time
i Waited, i Puzzled
my hand revealed through a feel:
my hair! it had grown! unreal!
crew cuts never last. you'd have thought me Samson
bring on the attack!

No one came; all stayed the same
except for me, i Bolted
i ran the mile, on a track of style
of gold and silver markings

in a lane lined gold, i stopped, then strolled out the
pewter archway
more becalmed, i skipped along on a hopscotch design
of ivory

You appeared, on a soccer field of astro-turf
and bleachers
i sat down, while you ran around
kicking a ball towards netting–
with resound, you sent it soundly down the line –
you made it!

i jumped and roared, "good shot! you scored!" but found
the field was vacant

That's the second time for *Lose and Find*
it really got quite boring
though with a shrug, i kept on searching
(a man does what he does!)

From the field, i should have yielded, though
something drove me on
the water's glare from a pool of grandeur
attracted me like fly to frog
(i'd have to be half manatee, to venture such a feat)

though i can't swim, i threw me in
and realized: i was sunk!

up for air, i fought to stay there

Flapping, as if a duck. You were there   way out there
fifty yards   or more

you raised a hand; i thought you'd seen me
surely, i was to be Saved
you waved your arm as if to signal,
"it's all right! you'll be OK!"

back and forth, your arm went dully: a railroad crossing
came to mind

why do you wait? my mind was screaming
and as i went under i heard your roar,
"That's two! That's two!" your voice came peeling
oh my God! you're keeping score!

The very next thing that i remember is
when i came to and looked around
it wasn't Heaven: i heard no trumpets; in fact, in death there
is no sound!

oh, i know you! i slowly realized
you're the place of no replies
just you ask for help, and see what happens
if you're drowning – then you'll die!

but then it came, a recognition, i was Alive
if still in Hell
she must have saved me – how i misjudged her
i sat awhile and took some rest

Once again, i started searching, in soggy clothes
(my shoes and socks felt as if they held the ocean)
i made my way – Curplop! Curplop!

coming upon a court (for tennis), i heard the
Scream of cat gut cries
Smashing hard, the racket sounded: an ace for sure!
my thoughts replied

it was her – i'm sure you knew it – i would have too
if i had tried
i smiled and sighed; i was glad to see her
to let her know i hadn't died!

"Hello!" i said, approaching. She waved as if,
Goodbye!

i went to speak, but i just stuttered
my nerves were shot, my clothes clung tight
finding speech, i finally sputtered a splattering talk
that spats in eyes

composure came, but so did dawning
with the light, no answers came
as i bathed, my thoughts did weaken
with a shave – Poof! they went away

Swiftly ... Swifter!

Embroiled in thicket branches
a gash cut in my leg
Woods in textured hues of gold
flash upon the graves

The land is lost in folding,
carpeted in fog
The moon is high
a bloody eye
that seers thoughts of souls

Quiet, cradles darkness
it strangles with its hold
All is dead, inside my head
(all but heartbeat's drone)

The underbrush is thinning now
my pace has quickened some
I move in step
my movements kept
in tempo with my hums

One false step, and i could loose it
i haven't very far to go
The smell draws nearer: of grass, of flowers
the riverbed; across is home!

The water numbs my spirit
my fears won't wash away
I fear i'll die; the tide will take me
thrashing, to my grave

Having struggled to the shore

i claw, i grasp, i pray,
i pull, i tug, i swear some now
my actions seem in vain

The air and water burn my wound
as i hoist me to the ground
The night is cold, colder
than it was before i drowned

Limping, i take off through the forest
at least i bleed no more
My blood's congealed
though pain's concealed
in every growling groan

Branches slow me down some
as they slash across my face
But i don't feel their whipping
and resume my noble pace

It's not until a wind blows
that sets my cheek to throb
By God! but that won't stop me
Swiftly! i go on

Exhaustion overtakes me
a gallant try, old man
I can feel the life of me
dissolve, as if of sand

Freedom's just a step now
maybe two or three
Hell! it's a mile!
but all the while
i lie on, just the same

Swiftly ... Swifter!
it approaches! up ahead!
The field of where my thoughts do steal to
hearkens as a friend

Smoke is rising from the chimney
the end is drawing nigh
I can't wait to see them
thank Heaven, i survived!

The cabin door is opened now
i didn't even knock!
The land is scanned and with his hand
the wind is lightly touched

I wasn't even noticed! What of me! i cry
Oh God! i scream in anger
it's really true – I died!

Lady Fair

I once dreamed of love, a queen
a vision in a mist

I was told she was to hold
that life was made for this

Approaching close, i did my most
to win her love and favor

"Love's not free," she hissed at me.
"what more have you to offer?"

I did my most, though not to boast
to please her with my answer

"I've love anew, and will care for you;
would not this be sufficient?"

"You'll give more!" she sneered and roared.
"Or find yourself another!"

"All i have, my Lady Fair," i stammered out my answer,
"is love unsworn,a heart untorn – a treasure for the taking."

"Is this all! Or do you stall?" she peered at me in anger
"Where's your gold? And wealth untold?
that you should have my passion!"

"I've no gold nor wealth untold," i shrugged, in my surmising.
"All i need i see in thee, in eyes so wide and knowing."

"What you see!" she scoffed at me. "Pity! And no more.
What you see!" she mocked in glee. "You really are a bore!

But do tell me more, you Silly bore, of love and of its folly."

"Lady Fair, love's so rare, so rare in its arriving;
wings of might soar in flight and fill the heart with fire."

She chuckled at me. "Fire! I see. My Word, you Silly boy."

"Fire! My Fair. And trumpet's blare!"

"You Silly, Silly boy! Don't be absurd!" her wide eyes scourged.
"Love is but a word; a facade, you see, that masks men's greed
Love? Huh! But a word! When you wake, your heart will ache
for wants and for desires. Then you'll see – your love
that's free – is not what flames your fire."

"It's beauty,Fair!" my protest blared. "Not what you would
make it."

"Beauty. Indeed! Tis pain and greed. Faith and trust forsaken."

"Tis like the air, my Lady Fair: sweet and life renewing."

"So This is life." Her words a knife. "May death consume
my marrow!"

"What could be so that gives one woe, one so fair,
so beckoning?"

"Tis love once claimed that bore my pain,
tis me who bears the sorrow."

"Lady Fair, fate's unfair, for you to bear its burden.
But wounds do heal through times repeal
and burdens bear much lighter."

"Silly boy! Life's not a toy built to suit your fancy."

"Lady Fair, it's not a tear that never knows a needle."

"There is no joy! Silly boy. It's all of pain and sorrow."

"No, Lady Fair, though not always fair: life is for the choos-
ing."

She beamed with joy, though as a ploy. "silly,silly boy."
Her voice sublime, ''You'd change my mind – or try with
time – but dawn is on the breaking. Do tell me more,you
silly bore, of love and of its losing. What have you,silly fool,
to do with pain and sorrow?"

"I've had my share, my Lady Fair," i said in pain's reprising.
"My heart's been torn. I've felt forlorned. I've felt my life
in ruins. Even so, one thing i know: misery loves its company."

"You Silly bore! You may wish more of love and its illusions
but this i swear: i've had my share. No more will i be broken."

"I hearken thee," my eyes did plead, "release you from
this prison. Set you free of thieves as these: of pain,
of hate, of sorrow."

"Depart from me! Then i'll be free. You silly, silly boy."

"Daybreak stares, my Lady Fair, is there nothing i can say? Free
your heart, and though we part, please, do not forget me."

She hissed annoyed. "Silly boy!" Her wide eyes peered,
unknowing

…i once had a dream of love, a queen
   a vision in a mist

All For Love

A Penny's Worth

The fountain calls
to one and all:
please, give to me a penny

and i will grant you
what you wish for
in your life of longing

copper coins of penny worth
dot my concrete basin
their value,   rare
for those who toss them there
a dream   a wish   a summons

The fountain calls
to one and all:
what have you to wager?

a penny cost is all
it costs you
to barter for your freedom

draw in nigh
and close your eyes
wish for what you're longing

take a chance
don't let one pass!
who says dreams are wasteful?

copper coins of penny worth
dot the concrete basin
mine shines there
a wishful glare:

hope costs but a penny!

RAINBOW'S END

They pass by signs like:
    Tudor Rose
    The Rainbow's End
    The Emporium

they're friendly calls
which beckon all
people pass each other

Flashing signs
enfold the mind
the old ones sit around them

passersby don't hear the sighs
they're indifferent
without malice

Those who grieve
and wear their sleeve
with their hearts laid down upon it
for those impaired
those not fair
their needs and wants aren't noticed

they wear no sign
and yet the blind!
could sense
the ruination

but pain won't glow
as Tudor Rose
and rainbow's end is missing

Thoughts of these
would surely mean
a loss of bliss-indifference

the mind would care
the heart would tear
for the soul
its loss of innocence

To those who bear
what won't be shared
for those who go unnoticed:
in a world serene inside its dreams

the neon's only noticed!

I Sit In Rest

Her steady stare
invites compassion
though you can tell
she asks for none

All she seeks
is recognition
a telling glance–
you're not alone!

Her fist wrapped 'round
a tie-top baggie
(used to hold the waste of some)
she holds it near
for unlike others
it's a womb
which carries love

She takes a seat
(across the fountain)
props her bag
upon the bench

Looks at me
in waxen wonder
her hand to chin
she sits in rest

All she needs
sits there beside her
it's all she's known
it's all she's had

A simple twist
removes the tie-on
the bag unfurls
in caring hands

With gentle strokes
she shares compassion
with her friend
of ready smile

A collie dog
of polyester
with sawdust soul
where love resides

She pats his head
returns the tie-on
once again her life's been blessed

As she leaves
i reflect in wonder
smiling faintly
to myself

for thoughts of her
are warm inside me
i'm not alone
i sit in rest

In a field reside two blooms
side by side
they reach for sky

Overhead, two birds of summer
circle high, throughout the sky

"If we were they,"
a bloom proclaims,
"we too could fly and soar the sky."

"It would be new,"
his friend bemuses,
"To take to sky with wings that fly."

"What have we?"
the first agrees
"We don't move! We're not free!"

"Agreed! my friend,
until the end
what have we? but what we see!"

From on high
the birds incline
their graceful motions
take the sky

"Look how free!"
the blooms decry
"Look how free!"
they watch the sky

"If that were we,"
the first invites,
"we would know more than just the sky."

His friend sighs in his seething
"We could know what flowers see!"

"Agreed! Agreed!
until the end for us will be
only that of which WE see!"

"Agreed! Agreed!"
his friend concedes.
"What the life these flowers lead!"

Through his cry,the first agrees
"What the life! Indeed! Indeed!
from the seed they rest and feed
never do they search for needs!"

Cutting sky, their wings deride
slashing 'cross the tie that binds them

Down below, the blooms bemoan
and keep their face towards heaven

SPIRITS OF NIGHT

our candles are lighted
our voices are raised
yet
not a hand holds a hand on this gathering day

carols are heralded,
"peace, fill the land!"
yet
we only sing them,with candles in hand –

their light shines upon us
our voices invite,
"love everybody!"
our spirits unite

our words, they come strong now
they fill the night air
and flicker our candles
our conscience is clear

without but a touch
we love (as we do)
only in spirit–
merry Christmas to you!

ALL FOR LOVE

His massive hoofs tread the ground
a rhythmic, nimble touch

Mighty tusks slash through silence
trumpeting, shatters calm

A call of rage! to disengage
to save his clan from slaughter

Shots ring 'round, he falls to the ground
it's all for love of ivory!

His face cut away, his tusks are weighed
life is just a measure–

For two hundred pounds they shot him down
all for love of money!

His carcass spared, it stinks the air
vultures leave their droppings

The suicide of humankind
leaves a shadow in the falling

As I Pass By

THE TRUTH OF LIGHT

i put my arm
'round her waist
she cups her hand
round mine

we walk along
the stars are bright
her touch is smooth and kind

the softness
of you
as i hold you
such as this, i've never known

though the night is cold and airy
in your arms
i lie in warmth

the grass is moist
(a quilt of dawning)
now's the time of purity –

if this be love
consume me! consume me!

sunbeams arch
o'er the treetops
the park awakens
from the night

strolling on
we face the sunrise
still i wonder (in my plight)

does love withstand
the truth of light?

IF YOU WANT TO

if you want to
give me
something

give me
something
of yourself:

a smile
a nod
a wink
a greeting

something that which
stores don't shelve

if you wish to
gain my
favor

tribute me in ways
as these
when your heart does
think of me:

a dandelion
a shining pebble
a maple leaf
a box of seeds

things of which in cost
mean nothing
still
my heart would
cherish these

if you want to say
i love you
that is easy
without words:

a look
a hug
a kiss
a handshake

one of these would say
to me
what your heart does think
of me

if i can
i'll win your
favor
i'll give to you all that
 i have:

my heart
my soul
my life
my feelings
my love for you

i cherish these!

AS I PASS BY

her legs are folded
under her
she sits there all
alone

she holds
a book
though as she reads
her eyes are glazed as
stones

snowflakes swirl
this springtime day
the air is brisk
enfolding

i pass by
though as i do
my eyes reply in kind

maple branches
call to me
they rustle in the wind

from the tree
she nestles under
they beckon as a friend

peering upwards
she scans the sky
looks ahead
and shutters

i reply with eyes of
longing
and make my way in
silence

EVERYWHERE I AM

what do you do alone at night?
i read a book by tranquil light

what do you do to clear your head?
sit and feel my hair grow in

why is it that you don't go out?
i did, once, but it was dark

don't you ever feel alone?
i am here.   my mind's not home

won't you ever change your ways?
 when i'm dead i'll have no say

is there nothing we can do?
...close the door as you leave the room

i like silence, sometimes
silence makes people nervous

(   )

see what i mean
makes them jumpy

what's the matter:
why are you upset they wonder

silence may be golden
but it can't be worth very much
no one seems to want any.

(   )

WHEN IT RAINS...

She was the love
of my life
she encompassed
my world

my existence to her
meant nothing, i'm sure
(though hope: it rings eternal)

One cloudy morning
i hopped on my bike
made my way to her
the love of my life
on a pathway of dirt and of stones

rain began falling
(isn't that always the way!)
it never turns on you
but on such a day

Mud began forming
an oozing decay
i pedaled on harder
i failed in the strain

it came with the struggle
dirt clots unfurling
splattering o'er me

What's there to do now?
love's not denied
by God i shall carry it!
it poured down unkind

soon it let up
soon – not before
soon wasn't soon enough
i was soaked to the core
as i trudged on through the muck

At the bandstand
not far from her house
i huddled in silence
the rain beat a waltz

what's there to do now?
by God! i've come far
courage is climaxing
indeed O so far

The shower soon slackened
soon it subsides
i take to my steed
off! i do ride

upon my arrival
i pace by the drive
never before have i felt so alive!
and lonely

Having arrived
i rap on the door
(maybe a tap)
i knock that much more

the door opens, slowly
parts barely a crack
an eye ponders deeply
staring aghast

She stands here before me
her daughter is home
yes, she'll go get her
my heart beats in throngs

she stands here before me
the air that i breathe
yes, she is near me
the love of my dreams

A mouthful of bile
i'm sorry she says
the door closes firmly
by god, it's the end

i stand as a statue
the axis of time
it circles around me
though movement declines

The sun begins warming
the clouds drift away
my clothes will soon lighten
the mud will leave stains
(isn't that always the way)

SOMETHING ABOUT MY TRUE LOVE

We have this clock
that works
sporadically

but it is ours

of our shared
history

We tend it
as a friend

we don't mind
what others say

– She's comfortable
that way

THOUGH & YET

I'm alone, though all are near me
you are near, yet, i'm alone

i could cry, though i am empty
nothing fills, yet, teardrops fall

i can see, though i'm in darkness
there is light, yet, night is known

i should speak, though no one asks me
no one speaks, yet, they call

i can touch, though touch means caring
yes, i care, yet, i don't touch

i should smile, though i've no feeling
nothing moves me, yet, i frown

i do give, though receiving's harder
much too hard, yet, i am bound

i will love, though i'm a poor man
love is free, yet, i have paid

i am strong, though heartache weakens
i am tired, yet, strength has stayed

i will live, though there's no reason
death is easy, yet, i will stay

the world is mine, though i am drifting
i'm an island, yet, all is me

...create a twisted world
you're bound to come out twisted

HE STANDS BEFORE ME

i see the boy before me
i wonder who he sees

the man that stands before him
alone inside his grief?

i see the boy before me
his faith still comforts me

he looks back through the mirror
i wonder
does he grieve?

Imagine That

...pitty-patt (imagine that)
the cow jumped over the moon

too soon   too soon   (silly moon)

make believe that you are sane
silly game   silly game

keep your mind from death's refrain
silly game   silly game

hickory, dickory, dock
                ,
                h
                a
                n
                g

                y
                o
                u
                r
                s
                e
                l
                f

                f
                r
                o
                m

                a

                c
                l
                o
                c
                k

if the clock falls down continue on
by the light of the silvery moon
too soon   too soon   (silly moon)

a pocket full of lye
take it by the handful

shrivel up and die
say goodbye to life

Old Mother Hubbard
lives in a cupboard (or is it in a shoe)

she was Damn frustrated
what to do, what to do

i am coming too
too soon   too soon

what's that wrapping
tapping at my door

CURSE YOUR HIDE FOREVER MORE

too soon   too soon
she steps into the room

how's the kids
so you've flipped your lid!

don't you bother me
i am seeking peace

i almost knew the score
damn your kids! damn the door!

DON'T BOTHER ME FOREVER MORE

pease porridge hot, pease porridge cold
the lye in my stomach is boring a hole

silly ass
you'll not die fast

There once was a girl from Nantucket
Oh Hell   somebody   Bring Me a bucket!

the cupboard is bare
i'll puke through the air

...and frightened Miss Muffet away
delays – never have neighbors, it pays

It's Howdy Doody Time!
Oh Hell   i'm almost out of rhyme

lye burns deep in me
it's now a part of me

ta-ra-ra-boom-de-aye!

i feel a sudden pain
not like i've known before

i think my time has flown

But let's have another cup of coffee
and let's have another piece of pie

Oh Hell, that lye

Damn Its Eyes!
The Moon Is In The Seventh Planet
I've Had It! I've Had It!

Jack B. Nimble, Jack B. Quick
whatever you do – Don't Blow It!

Forgive Us Our Trespasses
but never make passes at girls who wear glasses

(Forgive me Dorothy Parker
for martyring your poem)

go home   go home

Be it ever so humble
don't start to bumble

Silly Fool   obey the rules

live to die another day
what's in a name, except a name

Smoke Gets In Your Eyes
when your heart's of lye

Silly Fool   obey the rules

Rub-a -dub-dub...
Ah, There's The Rub!

i could drown myself inside the tub
but the Old Man In The Sea

took my plug from me

Silly Ass, the plug won't last
Nearer My God To Thee he'll Be
when it pops out and rides the sea

maybe he will try to see if man can really fly

he will find somebody new
but what am i to do

I've Got No Plug, Got No Sea
but i've the Sun in the morning

the Moon at night
Bess is my Woman though i must look a fright

Who Could Ask For Anything More
damn the door (i had to ask)

Come right in Miss Sassafras!
don't need no water, please

a plug would serve my needs
Come To Me! Come To Me!

What's That You Say
you're Nurse –

go away! go away!

you woke me from my dream
i almost walked on sea

that Old Man yet
he owes me

i almost Knew Of God
(behind the cool facade

     never mind the man behind the curtain

Truth is in the clouds
                beyond the reach of knowledge

somewhere over the Rainbow
i barely missed it, still

a kiss is still a kiss so let us not remiss
kiss me once, kiss me twice

some advice before you go
there's nothing up my sleeve)

i've but this to speak –

please don't walk away
not before i say –

what's that about the meek
you've a lot of Cheek

quoting me a poem
when i do speak of Freedom

Then Be Off With You
silly fool

he who will not see is
blinder than a dream

or something such as that

I Must Get Back! I Must Get Back!
someone knocks for me
Could It Be   Could It Be

first, before you go
Let Yourself Go! Let Yourself Go!

and if you're heading 'cross the river
before washing your sins away in the tide

tell The Old Man: the plug!
or else He Surely Dies

oh never mind, never mind

good night SweetHeart
dream will banish sorrow

Old MacDonald's on the phone?
could you hold it 'til

tomorrow
parting is such sorrow (sweet though it may be)

someone Knocks for me
could it be   could it be

REFLECTIONS OF ME

REFLECTIONS OF ME

What do i see when i look at me?
a man bewildered by what he sees
        bemuddled
        befuddled
        beriddled
        beware! ... of those whose words echo declares of:
        friendship
        passion
        how are you? ... much too blue to talk with you

What is thought by a fool like me?
do i think? do i see?
        pleasure?
        love?
        life's there too! ... but not for me – i'm much too blue

What is felt by one so numb?
        kisses?
        touches?
        peace? (now come!)
        nothing is felt, but what to do?
        i can't care, i'm much too blue

What is left for me to do?
        slit my throat?
        go turn blue?
        suicide could cure the blues – but i'm too blue to do
        that too!

        One day when all is said and done
        i will turn blue, i'll be as one
        but i can't think of that today
        'cause if i do
        ...i might feel gay!

CIRCLE ROUND

run! young man … keep running!
'round the tile you go
circling, may tire with age
run! before you slow

run around … shout!
fall down
you will get back up
there's nothing there to keep you down
hope will keep you up

circle! circle! like a top
never mind what for
let yourself go, freely, with it
for when you stop
time's flown!

In The Land of Opportunity

violence is the mother tongue:
Hey! You! Get off my island!

Life of peace? for deceased!
go and try to get you some

Hey! You! Boy! there is no joy
make yourself a white man
change your plight from black to white
go and try to get you some

Hey! You! There! your views, impaired
we don't need your comments
in this land, the group commands
go and try to find you one

Hey! You! There! who screams: UNFAIR!
you only get what's coming
we've our share – so yours is spare?
go and try to get you some

Hey! You! There! you're abused? who cares!
keep it to yourself
life is tough ... it takes some guts!
go and try to get you some

A Peasant's Dream

Spring's freeing fragrance
a shining star
a path to guide the way

could one sight capture all of this?
are peasants ever king?

An autumn kiss
a warming flame
a chance for faith restored

can one sweet smile be all of this?
and heart's hope bring much more?

A longed for touch
a needy heart
the soul of pain's reprise

is there not hope for one like me
for one the fates despise!

But through a look i see in you
what you can't see in me
for i have learned that in this world

the peasant's never king!

HELLO   GOODBYE

i could have spoken
what would i have said?
still, it had ended, surely
before you began

what does it take, to share a smile?
converse with someone? to care for awhile?

you said, "hello." i grinned, goodbye.
our conversation wasn't wide,
what was i reading?
i spoke the words
you needed more than hollow words

you turned away. i felt alone.
my shield was broken. i was alone.

your presence cut me in its need
you walked away. my heart did bleed.

WALKING ON A PIER IN WINDY WEATHER

water sounds around
me

(as in the womb
it soothes my soul)

would that i could know
once again, its hold

whitecaps burst
as fireworks

against the breaker-wall

sprays
of moonlit sun

shower forth as water blossoms
their season to abide –

the blinking of an eye

WINTER SUNSET

the denouement
of day

splashes 'cross the pane of heaven

pastels
pink and blue

of bright
and shadowed hue

paint a scene
of mystic wonder

on wings of darkness soar

spirits of the night
imploring

coursing 'cross the span of heaven

in their wake
ignite

sparks
of starlight

A DARWINIAN PARADOX:

sea gulls

(en masse
 upon the sand)

clustered, in their need
for others; life is never known

encumbered

FOR THOSE WHO WRITE

i sit, alone, and write here
why? i'll never know
pretty girls parade by me
their style: a fashion show

you would think me quite the ancient one
a fad now past my time
but just the same, i'm not to blame
if i can't catch an eye

each man is famous, for awhile
(the saying maybe goes)
but one must live
and take what's his
before he's ever known

possessions are nine-tenths of life
(or so i think some say)
one plus one... or so when it's done
for me, comes out the same: one

back to fame, for just a while
they say it's in the name
but i can't figure what they mean
to me a name's a name!

nothing ventured, nothing gained
(this one, i got right!)
nothing gained still remains:
what *i* get when i try

live it, before it's over
(i just made that up)
Even so, the words ring true –
except for those who write!

I have watched clouds,
walked in the rain,

heard leaves in gentle sway
in windswept woods,

(i've prayed
 in my own way)

I've beheld the essence
of life's soul

felt its healing hold
in my time i've come to know:

nothing ever ends

i will not, my friend
i shall linger

as a song
a windswept sweet reprise

listen, and you'll know of me

As raindrops
i will beckon

life within its seed
(all are part of me)

let me share with you my meaning

I will amble
as a cloud

(what i've sought for
 i have found)

anywhere i am is freedom

if to the truth
i'm bound

I, too, have gazed
at stars at night

and felt their measure
chart my soul

with God's own guiding light
i tell you that it's true –

because i know of me
my friend

i do know of you!